VIRGO

A GUIDED JOURNAL

Constance Stellas

ADAMS MEDIA
New York London Toronto Sydney New Delhi

Adams Media
An Imprint of Simon & Schuster, Inc.
100 Technology Center Drive
Stoughton, Massachusetts 02072

First Adams Media hardcover edition September 2022

ADAMS MEDIA and colophon are trademarks of Simon & Schuster.

For information about special discounts for bulk purchases, please contact Simon & Schuster Special Sales at 1-866-506-1949 or business@simonandschuster.com.

The Simon & Schuster Speakers Bureau can bring authors to your live event. For more information or to book an event contact the Simon & Schuster Speakers Bureau at 1-866-248-3049 or visit our website at www.simonspeakers.com.

Interior design by Colleen Cunningham
Interior illustrations by Tess Armstrong
Interior images © Getty Images/Vikiss, Mara Fribus; Simon & Schuster, Inc.

Manufactured in China

10 9 8 7 6 5 4 3 2 1

ISBN 978-1-5072-1958-4

CONTENTS

INTRODUCTION

Are you interested in how the stars may influence your characteristics? Wanting a little celestial insight into how you can strengthen your relationships? Looking for guidance in using your analytical and hardworking skills? Guided journaling can be a dialogue between your thoughts, feelings, and aspects of your sign and element. By reflecting in an intentional way, you can begin to understand yourself—and how you interact with the world around you—better.

An earth sign, Virgo is the last personal sign of the zodiac (personal signs each have a purpose in developing a soul's personality). Virgo's purpose is to give service and care to others. Journaling can help you discern how to give this service and care—not only to others but to yourself as well. Do you feel fulfilled when helping someone? Or drained when you neglect caring for yourself? The prompts in this book will allow you to cultivate more ease in pursuing your astrological path, and for everyday life, by exploring your Virgo tendencies and what you may share with other earth signs.

Journaling can also help you be in touch with how you feel about situations and people rather than getting stuck in analyzing what is happening or thinking about people's motivations. Virgo is symbolized by the maid who plans, plants, and cultivates the food people need to live. Likewise, Virgo has a natural talent for hard work and organizing whether she is planting the crops or analyzing a spreadsheet for her employees. The shadow side of these analytical abilities, however, is criticism. Virgo can feel that no one or nothing is good enough. Fixating on present worries? Feeling like you fail whenever things don't turn out "perfect"? By reflecting on the prompts in this book, you'll gain a deeper understanding of what has and hasn't helped you effectively use (or calm) your analytical brain and learn how to create a more integrated, focused future.

When you write, you connect with your feelings, desires, and everything in between. And when prompts drive you to contemplate the wealth of astrological wisdom that each element and Sun sign offers, it can lead to surprising, creative insights. Maybe you recognize your need to master materials and analyze everything, but you may not be aware of exactly how you can put this detail-oriented ability to use in any endeavor, be it work, partnership, or love. Or perhaps you never considered how practices such as meditation could help you quiet your worried thoughts. This book will help you explore yourself and your place among the stars.

HOW TO USE THIS BOOK

Welcome to your astrology journal! This guided journal is divided into three parts to help you explore your connections to the stars.

PART ONE

First, there are prompts about astrology in general, from how you feel about astrological wisdom to what you notice about your relationships with different signs and your experiences with reading horoscopes. The long and rich history of astrology can truly enhance your life and deepen your self-knowledge. Whatever strikes your fancy is a prompt to pursue! The purpose is not to master celestial knowledge but to turn your thoughts to the cosmos and reflect in an intentional way that may uncover some surprising insights.

PART TWO

The second part features prompts about your element. In astrology, there are four elements:

- Fire
- Earth
- Air
- Water

There are three zodiac signs in each element.

THE PASSIONATE FIRE SIGNS ARE:	ARIES	LEO	SAGITTARIUS

THE PRACTICAL EARTH SIGNS ARE:	TAURUS	VIRGO	CAPRICORN

THE COMMUNICATIVE AIR SIGNS ARE:	GEMINI	LIBRA	AQUARIUS

THE EMOTIONAL WATER SIGNS ARE:	CANCER	SCORPIO	PISCES

All members of the same element have an affinity; being with your elemental brothers or sisters can often feel comfortable because they speak your language. Understanding the characteristics of your element can give insight into good health practices and ways to relax and recharge, as well as how you might approach aspects of life such as work and relationships.

PART THREE

Finally, the third part of this journal concentrates on your Sun sign. This is the position of the sun when you were born. The Sun sign is a dominant feature in a person's entire chart. It reveals your:

- Psychological characteristics
- Health habits
- Relationship affinities
- Spiritual mission in this lifetime

Each Sun sign also has a ruling planet that gives the sign a certain kind of energy; a symbol that represents the characteristics of the sign's personality; and a modality that reveals whether that sign charges ahead in life, prefers the security of things remaining the same, or is open to the changes that come along. Consider these prompts intuitively. When something speaks to you and you think "Yes! That's me," reflect on the questions and any suggestions posed by the prompt. If you don't feel particularly drawn to a prompt, you may want to return to it later. If the information or questions in a prompt make you feel uncomfortable, consider whether there is something hidden or suppressed in your life that it awakens. Or you may use the page to explore why this doesn't fit you. True, not every aspect of the Sun sign will resonate with every person, so you may want to look at your full birth chart to help color the portrait of you that you create in this journal.

Astrology has become more and more popular, thanks to the ease of calculating birth charts online; the availability of daily, weekly, or monthly horoscopes delivered straight to your inbox; popular lists of famous people according to their Sun signs; and more. Ancient astrologers may have appreciated these options, *but* a computer is not a person, and the information that computer printouts offer is standard. Anyone born on the same day, time, year, and place as you would have the same astrology chart; however, people are individuals. There's a lot more to you than what is written about a Sun sign or astrological element. The beauty of this journal is that you can reflect on what astrology means to *you* and understand the nuances of your sign and element and how they do or don't relate to you as a unique person. Use this journal as your guide in exploring what the stars can teach you about yourself!

Astrology is the study of star and planetary patterns and what they mean for individuals and societies. Observing the regular motions of the sun, the moon, and other planets, ancient people became adept at interpreting what these celestial bodies and cycles meant. Today, there is a new renaissance in astrology, thanks to the Internet. Now anyone can find out the locations of the sun, the moon, Venus, and more at the time of their birth in just seconds, and subscribe to a service featuring daily, weekly, and monthly astrological forecasts. Consulting astrologers also offer star wisdom for health, business dealings, romance, spiritual development, and marriage.

In this part, you'll find thought-provoking prompts to guide you in reflecting on astrology in a more general context, rather than focusing on one specific sign or element. The sun, the moon, Mercury, Venus, Mars, Jupiter, Saturn, Uranus, Neptune, and Pluto: All of these celestial energies make up a natal chart and become a blueprint for gaining deeper self-knowledge and guiding your life. You can explore the astrological patterns in your family, track how different events like eclipses and equinoxes impact your mood and experiences, consider your beliefs on fate versus free will, and more. Enjoy this journey into the cosmos.

PART ONE

GETTING TO KNOW THE WORLD OF ASTROLOGY

Imagine you are lying on the grass or a beach or sitting on a bench at night. You can see the stars, perhaps the moon. Depending on the time of year, you might even see Venus twinkling on the horizon or a distant red glow from Mars. Describe what you feel. Awe? Like you are part of the universe? Or like you are insignificant compared to the vast celestial sky? Maybe curious to know more about the heavens?

....
....
....
....
....
....
....
....
....
....
....
....
....
....
....
....
....
....
....
....
....
....

If you were an ancient navigator and only had the constellations and the moon with which to navigate your ship to get home, would you feel comforted by the regularity of the patterns in the night sky? Write about a time when you felt lost literally or emotionally. Did the moon or a twinkling star give you courage? Did you notice if the moon during that time was just a crescent or full? Or maybe it was somewhere in between?

....
....
....
....
....
....
....
....
....
....
....
....
....
....
....
....
....
....
....
....
....

Astrology has become more and more popular in recent years, thanks to the Internet! Do you believe that everything astrology says about your sign is true? Write about a positive experience you have had reading your horoscope. Did you follow the advice? What happened?

....
....
....
....
....
....
....
....
....
....
....
....
....
....
....
....
....
....
....
....
....
....
....
....

What charms you about astrology? What bothers or concerns you about it? Are you mindful of the monthly zodiac sign changes? Describe any feelings you have about how certain zodiac time periods affect you. For example, in spring, when the sun is in Aries, maybe you feel energized.

Are there certain signs with which you are more harmonious? Less
harmonious? Write about your experiences.

....

....

....

....

....

....

....

....

....

....

....

....

....

....

....

....

....

....

....

....

....

....

....

....

....

....

....

A person's fate or destiny is a lifelong path. Describe how you feel when you read an astrological prediction for your future. Do you think it is good to know this information? Or better not to know? Do you use this information, keep it in mind, or ignore it?

....
....
....
....
....
....
....
....
....
....
....
....
....
....
....
....
....
....
....
....
....
....
....
....

Each zodiac sign is ruled by a planet or by the Sun or the Moon. Do you identify with Mercury, Venus, Mars, Jupiter, Saturn, Uranus, Neptune, Pluto, the Sun, or the Moon? Is it the planet your sign is ruled by? If not, describe your feelings about your own sign's planet. Do you think knowing more about your planet brings you insights into your personality or fortune?

....
....
....
....
....
....
....
....
....
....
....
....
....
....
....
....
....
....
....
....
....
....

The most famous—or infamous!—astrological event is Mercury Retrograde. This happens three times each year and means that Mercury appears to be moving backward in relation to the earth's orbit. It is common during these periods to experience electronic mishaps, communications going awry, and difficulties and delays in scheduling. Describe any Mercury Retrograde experiences you may have noticed. Were you forced to be more patient than usual?

If your Sun is in Gemini or Virgo, both signs ruled by Mercury, you may experience more personal confusion during Mercury in retrograde. Describe any personal confusion that you or your Gemini or Virgo friends experience at this time. Did you notice that you or they felt relief when Mercury was no longer retrograde?

....
....
....
....
....
....
....
....
....
....
....
....
....
....
....
....
....
....
....
....
....
....

The moon is our closest celestial neighbor, and its rhythms influence daily life. The monthly new moon marks the beginning of the moon's phases. At the new moon, people make wishes or set intentions with support from the moon's increasing energy as she waxes toward the full moon (the peak of lunar energy). Do you tend to notice the moon's phase, influence, or sign? Write about your relationship with and feeling toward this light.

Many astrologers believe that a person's chart can indicate past lives. What historical time period do you feel connected to? Who do you feel you might have been in a past life? What was your profession? Do you believe a past life can influence your present life? If so, how?

....
....
....
....
....
....
....
....
....
....
....
....
....
....
....
....
....
....
....
....
....
....
....
....

Each astrological sign is either masculine or feminine. This designation has nothing to do with gender or sexual orientation. The masculine signs radiate outwardly, and the feminine signs inwardly. Make a list of all the signs in your birth chart. Which energy dominates? Or perhaps they are equal? Do you feel these descriptions are true to your self-image?

....

....

....

....

....

....

....

....

....

....

....

....

....

....

....

....

....

....

....

....

....

....

In astrology, each sign has a symbol associated with it. Think about the symbol for your sign. Explore your feelings toward this symbol. Do any of its characteristics apply to you? You might write a story about yourself and what your symbol means to you. For example, as a Leo, are you more like a roaring lion or a purring cat?

As you will discover in this guided journey, there are four elements: fire, earth, air, and water. Each sign belongs to one element. Have you noticed that the signs of people you get along with have the same element as you do? Or a certain different element? Write about your experiences with people of the same and different elements.

Some people believe that following astrology curtails free will by forecasting the future. Do you believe this? Do you think it is possible that by knowing about your sign and using the stars as guides for the future you can make better choices in your life? Or do you feel controlled by what the stars say? Reflect on your feelings about free will and the stars.

Throughout the history of astrology, healers and physicians were required to study the positions of the planets in order to help their patients. They believed that the planetary energies could help or hinder healing the soul and body. What do you think about this idea? Can you implement any of your astrological insights into your health practices?

....
....
....
....
....
....
....
....
....
....
....
....
....
....
....
....
....
....
....
....
....
....
....

The position of the sun, the moon, and the ascendant are the three most important placements in a person's natal chart. If you know your birth time, you can easily determine these with the help of an app or astrology website. Explore your astrological trio and write down your feelings about these placements. Do you feel more connected to your moon or to your ascendant? Are there any patterns you notice, like the same element for each placement?

Eclipses were awesome phenomena for the ancients—and still have us in awe today! In a total solar eclipse, the sun's light is blocked by the moon, and the atmosphere darkens. In a lunar eclipse, the moon is blocked by the earth, and we cannot see this silvery orb. Most years have four eclipses. Do you pay attention to this heavenly event? Do you notice any patterns, either within yourself or in your surroundings during an eclipse? Research when the next eclipse will be, and record your feelings for the week leading up to the event.

....
....
....
....
....
....
....
....
....
....
....
....
....
....
....
....
....
....
....
....
....
....

How do you typically "use" astrology? Do you find it useful for
self-understanding? Understanding other people? Exploring your
friendships and/or partnerships? Do daily horoscopes guide your
actions? Or do you see astrology as more of a guide for larger
focuses in life? Write about an experience when an astrological tip
helped you in some way.

Have you noticed that people in the same family often have the same signs? Or that other positions in their charts correspond? It's frequently the case! Take a look at your family's and extended family's signs, and reflect on the similarities and differences.

....
....
....
....
....
....
....
....
....
....
....
....
....
....
....
....
....
....
....
....
....
....
....
....
....

Saturn is the farthest planet you can see with the naked eye. It rules time, structure, and lessons of life. A major astrological transit is the Saturn Return, when Saturn returns to its natal chart position. This happens between ages twenty-eight and thirty. Where is Saturn in your chart? Have you experienced this return? Whether you have experienced your Saturn Return or not, write about your feelings toward the current path of your life, relationships, health, and spiritual development. If you have experienced your Saturn Return, how did your life look during these years?

Aside from your Saturn Return, another important transit (when a planet returns to its original position in your birth chart) is with the planet Jupiter. Jupiter is called the benefic of the zodiac. He helps us feel generous toward ourselves and others, is good for business, and can bring new areas of creativity into life. Jupiter returns to his birthplace every twelve years. Think about your birthday years at each twelfth year so far. Write about your feelings and activities in those years. Were the experiences positive? Expansive? Creative?

The solstices, summer and winter, occur at opposite signs: Cancer in the summer, and Capricorn in the winter. They mark the height of sunlight in summer and the depths of darkness in winter. How is your mood at these times? Describe how these essential astrological markers affect you.

....
....
....
....
....
....
....
....
....
....
....
....
....
....
....
....
....
....
....
....
....
....
....
....

Two major points in nature and the celestial calendar are the equinoxes: the fall equinox (Libra) and the spring equinox (Aries). These events mean there is equal daylight and darkness during that day. Do you have any particular feelings during these times of the year? Happy fall is coming after a hot summer? Or anticipating spring after a harsh winter? Write your feelings about the rhythm of nature and how it corresponds to your experience of the seasons. If you live in the southern hemisphere, the equinoxes are reversed.

If someone you know says, "I don't believe in astrology, it's rubbish," what do you say back? Write a dialogue between you and a skeptical person. What are your points of agreement? Of disagreement?

....
....
....
....
....
....
....
....
....
....
....
....
....
....
....
....
....
....
....
....
....
....
....
....
....

Have you ever noticed that some days feel lucky and positive and that during other days nothing seems to go right? It could be that the planetary pattern in the sky is not in harmony with your personal planets! Keep a record of good and bad days and the placements of the planets during each day. Reflect on any patterns. (You can find the daily position of the planets online.)

Throughout history, people have sought to understand the world around them. Today we have scientific equipment to inform us of the makeup of the universe, but ancient peoples could only observe the basic elements that they saw in their lives: fire, earth, air, and water. They associated each of these elements with an astrological sign and certain characteristics, and physicians used these characteristics to treat and heal their patients. The elements and their characteristics are:

FIRE (Aries, Leo, Sagittarius): Fire signs are known for their passionate energy and impetuosity. They often need to moderate their bursts of enthusiasm to prevent burnout.

EARTH (Taurus, Virgo, Capricorn): Earth signs are practical, cautious, and seek out security with a measured pace. Cultivating change and taking a few risks can enhance their lives, boost their health, and encourage flexibility.

AIR (Gemini, Libra, Aquarius): Air signs are changeable and mentally oriented; they enjoy living in creative possibilities and have highly sensitive nervous systems. Getting "down to earth" can help air signs move forward realistically.

WATER (Cancer, Scorpio, Pisces): Water is the element of feelings, and all water signs react to life emotionally. Calming their waves of emotion in order to see a situation clearly is a lifelong challenge for all water signs.

The more than two dozen prompts in this part of the book will give you a platform for understanding more about yourself and your nature based on your element.

GETTING TO KNOW YOUR ELEMENT

Earth is our most familiar element. It is where we live and where we are connected to the practical aspects of life. "Be grounded," "feet on the ground," "down-to-earth": These are all expressions of the earth's hold on us. Write about your feelings regarding Planet Earth. Do you feel connected here? Happy in the place where you live?

There are many myths in different cultures about the creation of the earth. Most feature a Mother Earth figure, like Mother Nature. In Greek mythology, Gaia is the Earth Mother who emerged from cosmic chaos and gave birth to Ouranos, the sky god. "Protecting Gaia" is an expression used by modern ecology and environmental students to describe the interrelatedness of all plants, animals, minerals, and humans on Earth. Write your impressions about how people are currently interacting with Gaia. Are you involved in any groups related to helping the planet? Do you have a personal feeling about our home, Gaia?

Earth signs are levelheaded, concrete thinkers, and pragmatic. They favor practical solutions to problems. They like to measure success and progress. Does this describe you? How do you measure success and progress?

....
....
....
....
....
....
....
....
....
....
....
....
....
....
....
....
....
....
....
....
....
....
....
....

Earth is the element most associated with agriculture. A garden, vegetable patch, or fields of grain are all bounty from the earth! Do you garden? Grow plants? Describe any experiences you have had with agriculture or house plants. Do you have a favorite way to connect to agriculture or horticulture?

....

....

....

....

....

....

....

....

....

....

....

....

....

....

....

....

....

....

....

....

....

....

Earth signs—unlike the idea-oriented air signs, the passionate fire signs, or the fluid water signs—want to know "how do we accomplish our project?" Imagine you are the earth team leader with an air, fire, and water sign on your team. How do you gather the team to work together? How do you own your leadership role? Describe your plan for getting things done.

The seasons of spring, summer, autumn, and winter are the natural calendar and rhythm of the earth. Which season do you feel most connected to? Describe your feelings about this season, as well as the remaining seasons. Are there any special activities that you do in your spare time during each season?

Different areas of the earth bring out different feelings in people. Which areas do you prefer—urban or rural? Mountains or deserts? What climate suits you the best? What kinds of climates have you lived in, at different times of your life? Which place was/is the most comfortable?

....
....
....
....
....
....
....
....
....
....
....
....
....
....
....
....
....
....
....
....
....
....
....

In astrology, there is a technique called astrocartography. In this technique, the astrologer overlays a person's natal chart on a world map to see where harmonious and inharmonious locations are. Interesting! Where do you imagine your harmonious zone is? Are there any places that have been difficult to live in or visit? Concentrate on your feeling about the geography rather than the people.

....
....
....
....
....
....
....
....
....
....
....
....
....
....
....
....
....
....
....
....
....
....

Building—whether bridges, homes, churches, or monuments—is an earth activity. This is the way humans protect themselves from weather or celebrate the beauty of architecture and progress. Imagine the most beautiful, practical, and useful building you can. What would it look like? Where would it be? Write down your vision and how you might go about building this structure.

....
....
....
....
....
....
....
....
....
....
....
....
....
....
....
....
....
....
....
....
....
....
....
....
....
....
....
....
....

Caves with crystals, stalactites, and stalagmites run deep into the earth. Some caves even have rivers flowing through them! Have you ever visited a cave? Did you notice the peace and quiet? The cool, dark atmosphere? Write about any experiences you have had in caves. If you've never been to a cave, how do you feel about visiting one?

Crystals are nature's power sources from the earth. All crystals have a very steady rate of vibration. We mine them for our pleasure, their beauty, and to enhance our energy. Do you have a favorite type of crystal? A favorite crystal color? Write about your relationship with any crystal(s) you may have.

Native cultures are very particular about taking crystals out of the earth. They do not use bulldozers and seem to have a sixth sense of when a crystal mine has given up its rocks and needs to rest. Then they leave the earth alone. This natural rhythm can apply to all daily life: when to "harvest" and when to let the "field" lie fallow. Write about any experiences with this natural rhythm of sowing and reaping in any area of your life.

....
....
....
....
....
....
....
....
....
....
....
....
....
....
....
....
....
....
....
....
....

Gems are the most valuable and beautiful crystals the earth offers. Do you have a favorite gem? Describe it and any experiences you have had with this gem.

Each element personality has a characteristic type of humor! Dry wit and earthy jokes describe earth element humor. Is this true for you? Do you consider yourself a funny person? Describe your sense of humor and any occasions when you have entertained a circle of friends and/or family.

Earth sometimes blows her top with volcanoes or earthquakes. These tectonic shifts under the earth or sea balance the planet even though they can cause great damage in the process. Have you experienced an earthquake or volcano? Describe your feelings and experiences. If you haven't personally experienced an earthquake or volcano, what are your thoughts and feelings about them?

....
....
....
....
....
....
....
....
....
....
....
....
....
....
....
....
....
....
....
....
....
....
....
....

....
....
....
....
....
....
....
....
....
....
....
....
....
....
....
....
....
....
....
....
....
....
....
....
....
....
....
....
....

Just as the earth can erupt, we may sometimes find ourselves ready to burst with anger. Do you personally have temper eruptions? What kinds of situations enrage you? Write a dialogue between your calm self and that angry self.

Do you know that dogs and other animals sense earthquakes and other weather changes before they occur? Have you ever had a dog or other animal warn you of an upcoming weather event? If you are familiar with this "early-warning system," describe the event and what happened. If you have never had such an experience, how do you gather your weather information? TV weather? Smartphone app? *Farmers' Almanac?*

....
....
....
....
....
....
....
....
....
....
....
....
....
....
....
....
....
....
....
....
....
....

Trees are natural wonders that provide shade, clean the air, and give beauty. They can also provide a climate record of growth, drought, and famine. Trees form the backbone of the Wood Wide Web—a phrase that describes how trees communicate with each other to warn of pests and to help conserve water during dry seasons. Write about your experiences with trees. Have you ever visited an old forest?

The Wood Wide Web—the idea that trees can communicate with each other, send warnings about dangers, and help conserve water during a dry spell—is beautifully described in a book called *The Hidden Life of Trees* by Peter Wohlleben. If you've read this book, what were your thoughts? If you haven't read it, grab a copy and start reading, then write about your reactions.

....
....
....
....
....
....
....
....
....
....
....
....
....
....
....
....
....
....
....
....
....
....
....

Forest bathing—consciously walking, sitting, or lying down in a forest to feel the peaceful and healing atmosphere—has become popular in recent years. We want to connect with the earth and the trees. Have you ever done this? What were your experiences? If you haven't practiced forest bathing before, try it out, then write about how it went.

The pyramids are monumental structural achievements from ancient times. They were built by many different cultures, most famously in Egypt. Are you curious about how ancient people erected them without machines? Some people hypothesize that ancient people knew how to harden sand: They created frames on top of frames, filled them with sand, and let it harden. Very efficient! What do you think of this possibility? How do you think it connects with the characteristics of earth signs?

What is the most comfortable place in your home? Why? Did you build this home? Did you buy it? Or do you rent it? The earth element usually feels best owning their own home, so they can improve it without restrictions and increase its value. Write a dialogue between you and your home—the furniture, comforts, and discomforts. What have you improved? What would you like to improve?

....
....
....
....
....
....
....
....
....
....
....
....
....
....
....
....
....
....
....
....
....
....
....

People on Planet Earth often measure success by how much material wealth they garner. Do you believe this is the best measure of success? Is material wealth important to you? What other ways might you use to measure success?

....
....
....
....
....
....
....
....
....
....
....
....
....
....
....
....
....
....
....
....
....
....
....
....

Earth colors are warm beige, browns, burgundy, black, dark blue, and yellow. Are these your favorite colors? Describe your wardrobe: Is it full of earth tones? Do you wear different colors for different seasons?

If the ruler of the world were an earth sign, what would be their most important contribution? Would you nominate an earth, fire, air, or water sign to lead the world? Why?

If you were a highly developed being from another planet and landed on Earth, what would be your most significant observations about the land, resources, technology, and people? Do you believe there are more advanced civilizations than on Planet Earth?

The twelve astrological signs we know today come from the twelve constellations arranged around the ecliptic of the sun's path. Astrologers observe these signs and interpret their effect on people and events. For example, an astrologer may note that as a Virgo, a person might be great at analysis but find it challenging to synthesize all the details. And a Scorpio may be drawn to jobs or a certain career where they can investigate people or subjects, but a corporate structure doesn't appeal to them. Through understanding your Sun sign, you have a unique window of insight into yourself and your life!

The prompts in this part will guide you through a deeper exploration of your Sun sign and the traits, relationship dynamics, and more that may be influenced by this sign. Reflect on how your career path may be impacted by your sign. Consider how a certain characteristic linked to your sign plays into how you handle conflict with friends. Through guided journaling, this part will help you get to know yourself better. Of course, there is much more to astrology than your personal Sun sign. If you are interested in knowing even more about your relationship with the cosmos, you can also look at the other signs in your birth chart, such as your ascendant sign. Or you may want to focus more deeply on general astrology, as well as your Sun sign and sign element, and revisit different prompts to see how your reflections may evolve. This is *your* astrological journey: Let it take you wherever you want to go!

PART THREE

GETTING TO KNOW YOUR SIGN

Virgo is the second earth sign of the zodiac and one of only three signs whose symbol is human. She is the maiden gathering the harvest. The earth's bounty is Virgo's joy, and she pays attention to how the crops grow and all the details of cultivation. This trait has spilled over into her personality characteristics of paying attention to details and keeping order. Do you find this description applies to you? Reflect on the ways you feel this description does or doesn't line up with you. How do you feel when life is organized?

Virgo is a mutable sign. The mutable signs usher us from one season to the next; Virgo moves us from summer to autumn. Mutable signs are flexible and changeable, and Virgo is perhaps the most changeable of the earth signs! She adapts to whatever "gets the job done." Write about a time in your life when you had to be flexible to accomplish a project or goal.

Many Virgos believe their sign is problematic because they feel they must be perfect. Virgo does represent the quest for perfection, but the important word here is "quest," not "perfection." Write about a time when your creativity was challenged by your desire "to get everything right." Then write about a time when you were flexible and let go rather than following a rigid set of rules. Which approach benefited you the most?

....
....
....
....
....
....
....
....
....
....
....
....
....
....
....
....
....
....
....
....
....
....

As an earth sign, Virgo feels attached to the land and all manner of agriculture. Beekeeping is under Virgo's rulership. And like Virgo, these creatures are hardworking, bringing flowers and beauty to the land. Write about your experiences with plants or agriculture when you were a busy bee, improving the land or your life in general.

Along with a natural affinity for plants, Virgo has a good sixth sense for herbs and natural remedies for common ailments. Do you pursue the "natural way," if you have a health problem? Take a tonic in the winter to ward off colds? Or take herbs for overall health? Write about your experiences with natural remedies.

....
....
....
....
....
....
....
....
....
....
....
....
....
....
....
....
....
....
....
....
....
....
....
....

Work for Virgo usually involves analysis and attention to detail. She is meticulous in solving analytical problems and organizing teams to get the job done. Describe a time when you were the organizer and effortlessly put together a party or job project, or just cleaned out closets or other spaces in your own home and straightened up. Was it satisfying? Something that felt natural to you?

....
....
....
....
....
....
....
....
....
....
....
....
....
....
....
....
....
....
....
....
....
....

Despite being a sign of making order, there are messy Virgos! However, amid the chaos, Virgo almost always finds what she needs. If you are a messy Virgo, do you despair and try to clean up? Or just go with the flow? Describe your ideal home environment.

Virgo's ruler is Mercury, the planet of communication, mental activity, and messages. And yes, Mercury Retrograde can affect Virgo more than other signs. Do you notice when this planet is retrograde? Write about a time when you experienced communication or computer difficulties in a retro Mercury.

Mercury Retrograde can pose obstacles to effective communication and getting things done. But it can also be a freeing time, as it offers a chance for Virgo to set aside her desire for everything to be in perfect order. Write about a time during a Mercury Retrograde when you gave up the idea of order and perfection and tried going with the flow a little more. If you haven't tried this before, put it into practice during the next retrograde and record how it went.

Every sign rules a part of the body. Virgo rules digestion and the intestines. It is common for Virgo to have health complaints, most of which are related to worry and stress. Write about a time when your body rebelled due to stress and/or anxiety. What part of your body gave you trouble? Were you able to calm down and relax? If so, how? How did relaxing impact the situation? If not, what happened?

....
....
....
....
....
....
....
....
....
....
....
....
....
....
....
....
....
....
....
....
....
....

Meditation to counteract worry is a good practice for everyone and especially for Virgo, who can be prone to anxious thoughts. Do you follow any meditation practice? Describe your method and the times it has relaxed your mind and body. If you do not use meditation, explore different options and try one out, then write about how it went.

Virgo's ruler, Mercury, is a very mentally active planet and can lead Virgo into excessive worry. Describe a time (or multiple times) when your thoughts were in a whirl, and you couldn't calm down. What happened? What did you do to bring yourself peace?

....
....
....
....
....
....
....
....
....
....
....
....
....
....
....
....
....
....
....
....
....
....
....
....
....

Virgo is a planner. Whether the task is shopping for dinner or getting ready for a workday, Virgo feels confident if all things are in order and ready to go. Describe your daily rituals. Are they efficient? Are there changes you could make to make things even easier? If so, what?

....
....
....
....
....
....
....
....
....
....
....
....
....
....
....
....
....
....
....
....
....
....
....

Diet is important to Virgo due to their sensitive digestion. Usually, they avoid spices and prefer mild, simple, well-cooked food without heavy sauces. Describe your favorite meal. Does it comfort you? Do you like ethnic food? Or prefer your native cuisine? Do you like to get adventurous with meals or stick to what you know?

In the soul cycle of the zodiac, Virgo is the last personal sign...that is, a sign dedicated to developing parts of the personality. For Virgo, the soul is learning how to be of service to others. Of course, this is not at the expense of your own needs but is expressed in the satisfaction of being helpful. Write about what service means to you. Do you like providing service to others? Do you feel it is your purpose?

In relationships, Virgo can be picky. Having a partner who is sloppy, disorganized, or unconcerned with health is rare. Describe your partner, a past partner, or a partner you imagine being with, and write about their most important positive and negative characteristics.

Virgo has been called the bachelor sign, as they tend to marry later in life. Is this true of you? Or another Virgo you know well? Describe your current relationship status and how it works or doesn't work for you.

....
....
....
....
....
....
....
....
....
....
....
....
....
....
....
....
....
....
....
....
....
....
....
....

Getting stuck in the details of life, a relationship, or a project can be a Virgo stumbling block. It is important to think about the big picture too! Do you ever consider this? How we are all connected? Do you feel grateful for the expanse of the universe? Write about how your life fits in or doesn't fit in the web of connectedness through your family, friends, colleagues, or your generation.

For detail-focused Virgo, it can be enlightening to step back and look at a larger picture once in a while. It helps to see how she is not alone but part of an expanse of connection that spans all life. This can also include past lives. Do you have intimations of a life you lived in the past? In what period was your past life? Where were you, and what were you doing? If this doesn't apply to you, consider exploring more about past lives and reflecting on what you discover. One great resource is *Many Lives, Many Masters* by Dr. Brian Weiss.

Practicality is Virgo's middle name! She has the knack of seeing real-world solutions to challenges or problems without a lot of theoretical considerations. Do you feel you are a practical person? In what ways are (or aren't) you practical? Have you ever "saved the day" with a practical solution? If so, what happened?

In fashion, Virgos prefer solid earth tones in white, brown, black, and navy blue. Their style is classic. Describe your ideal wardrobe. What kind of clothes do you feel most comfortable in?

Emotions are typically the realm of water signs. Virgo, of course, feels but expresses her feelings in a concrete way. No blubbering, no upheavals—just a clear statement: "This is how I feel." Describe the last time you felt a strong emotion like anger. What provoked you? How did you resolve your feelings?

Virgo is picky toward others but can pick on herself too. Write about a time when you were so critical of yourself that you were blocked and couldn't move forward on a project, relationship, or plan. Conversely, write about a time when you were able to move forward without criticism and self-consciousness or self-doubt.

Accompanying Virgo's interest in health is a great sensitivity to scent and essential oils. Have you ever used a scent diffuser? Lavender and bergamot are two oils that are delightful and calming. Describe your experiences with these scents or others. In what ways do they calm you? Or energize you?

....
....
....
....
....
....
....
....
....
....
....
....
....
....
....
....
....
....
....
....
....
....
....

Peppermint tea is a natural and old-fashioned remedy for digestive problems (which Virgos are prone to). Consider drinking this tea with a meal or after you eat. Write about any experiences you have had with peppermint. How can you incorporate it into your home remedy regime?

....

....

....

....

....

....

....

....

....

....

....

....

....

....

....

....

....

....

....

....

....

....

....

Virgos are frequently drawn to cats. Do you have a cat? Or another pet? If so, describe your relationship with your pet. If you don't have a cat or other pet, would you like to? Imagine what your relationship with your pet might be, and what kind of pet you would have. How would you go about getting a pet?

ADDITIONAL RESOURCES

Websites and Other Digital Resources

www.alabe.com

www.astro.com

www.astrodienst.com

www.lunarium.co.uk

www.changingofthegods.com

App: Co-Star

Books

Astrology, Psychology and the Four Elements by Stephen Arroyo

The Astrology of Fate by Liz Greene

Sun Signs by Linda Goodman

Relationship Signs by Linda Goodman

If You Want to Write by Brenda Ueland

The Artist's Way by Julia Cameron

The Hidden Life of Trees by Peter Wohlleben

The Hidden Power of Everyday Things by Constance Stellas, Julie Gillentine, and Jonathan Sharp

Sex Signs by Constance Stellas

The Astrological Guide to Self-Care by Constance Stellas

How to Be an Astrologer by Constance Stellas

The Little Book of Self-Care by Constance Stellas

BIBLIOGRAPHY

Arroyo, Stephen. *Astrology, Psychology and the Four Elements.* Davis, CA: CRCS, 1975.

Arroyo, Stephen. *Relationships & Life Cycles.* Vancouver, WA: CRCS, 1979.

Donath, Emma Belle. *Have We Met Before?* Tempe, AZ: American Federation of Astrologers, 1982.

Forrest, Steven. *The Book of Neptune.* Borrego Springs, CA: Seven Paws, 2016.

Forrest, Steven. *The Book of Fire.* Borrego Springs, CA: Seven Paws, 2019.

Green, Jeffrey Wolf. *Pluto: The Evolutionary Journey of the Soul, Volume I.* St. Paul, MN: Llewellyn, 1985.

Green, Jeffrey Wolf. *Pluto: The Soul's Evolution Through Relationships, Volume II.* St. Paul, MN: Llewellyn, 1997.

Greene, Liz. *The Astrology of Fate.* York Beach, ME: Weiser, 1984.

Hickey, Isabel M. *Astrology: A Cosmic Science.* Sebastopol, CA: CRCS, 2011.

Oken, Alan. *Soul Centered Astrology.* New York: Bantam, 1990.

Sargent, Lois Haines. *How to Handle Your Human Relations.* Tempe, AZ: American Federation of Astrologers, 1958.

Tester, Jim. *A History of Western Astrology.* New York: Ballantine, 1987.

Yott, Donald H. *Astrology and Reincarnation.* York Beach, ME: Weiser, 1989.

DEDICATION

To all those seeking the wisdom in their stars.

ACKNOWLEDGMENTS

I would like to thank Karen Cooper and everyone at Adams Media who helped with this book. To Brendan O'Neill, Katie Corcoran Lytle, Laura Daly, Julia Jacques, Sarah Doughty, Jo-Anne Duhamel, Julia DeGraf, and everyone else who worked on the manuscripts. To Frank Rivera, Priscilla Yuen, Colleen Cunningham, and Tess Armstrong for their work on the book's cover and interior design. I appreciated your team spirit and eagerness to dive into the riches of astrology.

Unique ways to refresh and restore— personalized for your

ZODIAC SIGN!

PICK UP OR DOWNLOAD YOUR COPIES TODAY!